DARING EARTHQUAKE RESCUES

AMY WAESCHLE

Consultant:
Jackie White, Captain of Fire Investigations
and Homeland Security, Albuquerque Fire Department

CAPSTONE PRESS
a capstone imprint

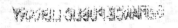

Edge Books are published by Capstone Press,
1710 Roe Crest Drive,
North Mankato, Minnesota 56003
www.mycapstone.com

Library of Congress Cataloging-in-Publication Data
Names: Waeschle, Amy, author.
Title: Daring earthquake rescues / by Amy Waeschle.
Description: North Mankato, Minnesota : an imprint of Capstone Press, [2018]
  | Series: Edge books. Rescued! | Audience: Age 8-14. | Includes
  bibliographical references and index.
Identifiers: LCCN 2017038588 (print) | LCCN 2017041289 (ebook) | ISBN
  9781543501223 (eBook PDF) | ISBN 9781543501148 (hardcover) | ISBN
  9781543501186 (paperback)
Subjects: LCSH: Earthquakes--Juvenile literature. | Rescues--Juvenile
  literature.
Classification: LCC HV599 (ebook) | LCC HV599 .W34 2018 (print) | DDC
  363.34/9581--dc23
LC record available at https://lccn.loc.gov/2017038588

Editorial Credits
Editor: Lauren Dupuis-Perez
Book Designer: Sara Radka
Production Specialist: Katy LaVigne

Quote Sources
p.9, "Buried in Haiti rubble, U.S. dad wrote goodbyes." Today, Jan. 19, 2010; p.14, "Deadly power of '94 quake was revealed at Northridge Meadows." *Los Angeles Times*, Jan. 17, 2014; p.17, "Italy earthquake: At least 73 dead, buildings destroyed as rescuers search for survivors." ABC, Aug. 24, 2016; p.20, "My 26 hours trapped." *New Zealand Herald*, Feb. 26, 2011; p.24, "Ecuador earthquake: 6.1-magnitude quake hits off coast days after deadly tremor." Independent, April 20, 2016; p.29, "Nepal earthquake: Teenager pulled alive from rubble on Day 6." CNN, May 1, 2015.

Image Credits
Getty Images: Berra1, back cover, Carl Court, 16, Feng Wei Photography, 27, Handout, 11, Hannah Peters, 7, 19, 20, Jonas Gratzer, 26, Omar Havana, 28, 29, schfer, 25, Taro Karibe, 4, U.S. Navy, 6, Uriel Sinai, 8, Wf Sihardian, 21; iStockphoto: ollo, 10, sengulmurat, 17; Newscom: ACG/NurPhoto/Sipa USA, 22, ANDES Xinhua News Agency, 24, Don Kohlbauer/U-T San Diego/ZUMAPRESS, 15, Joe Sohm Visions of America, 13, José Jácome/EFE, 23, Mark Mitchell/ABACAUSA, 18, Paul Harris pacificcoastnews, 12; Shutterstock: hxdbzxy, Cover

Graphic elements by Book Buddy Media and Capstone Press.

Printed and bound in the USA.
010780S18

Table of Contents

Rescues after Earthquakes

Earthquakes can break apart roads and cause landslides. A 7.3-magnitude earthquake destroyed a large section of a road in Kumamoto, Japan, in 2016.

Suddenly, the ground shakes. A loud rumble fills the air. Overhead lights sway. Walls begin to crumble and fall apart. It is an earthquake.

Every day, earthquakes shake the earth 500,000 times. Most are too small for people to feel. The bigger ones can be deadly. The biggest earthquake ever recorded happened in Chile in 1960. It killed more than a thousand people.

Earthquakes happen along the edges of Earth's **tectonic plates**. The tectonic plates form the outside layer of Earth, called the crust. They fit together like puzzle pieces. The plates are always moving. Where the edges meet, the plates slide over, under, or past one another. Even though the plates are made of rock, the rock can stretch to absorb the movement. But when the pressure becomes too great, the rock lets go. The sudden energy released creates an earthquake.

tectonic plate—a gigantic slab of Earth's crust that moves around on the mantle

The 2011 earthquake near Sendai, Japan, was the largest in the country's history. It caused a deadly tsunami that flooded towns.

Earthquakes can topple buildings, buckle roads, destroy bridges, and cause fires and landslides. When earthquakes happen on the seafloor, they can cause **tsunamis**. These giant waves can reach 100 feet (30 meters). These waves break on beaches around the world and destroy everything in their path.

Earthquake rescuers must work in dangerous conditions. They often have to make their way through broken buildings. Sometimes more earthquakes occur during rescue attempts. But the reward of saving someone's life makes it worth the difficulty. No rescue is the same, yet each requires bravery, determination, and hard work. Get ready to uncover earthquake rescue stories from around the world.

tsunami—a gigantic ocean wave created by an undersea earthquake, landslide, or volcanic eruption

Earthquake rescue workers must navigate dangerous piles of building materials while they work. They are always looking and listening for clues as to where a victim might be buried.

CHAPTER 1
Killer Quake Strikes Haiti

The 2010 Haiti earthquake destroyed more than 106,000 homes. The debris could have filled a line of train cars stretching for 2,500 miles (4,000 kilometers).

American volunteer worker Dan Woolley was inside his hotel in Port-au-Prince, Haiti, in January of 2010 when the floor started rolling under his feet. In seconds, Woolley was buried by broken walls as the hotel collapsed on top of him. When the shaking finally stopped, Woolley saw that he was stuck inside an elevator shaft. **Debris** boxed him in from all sides.

Woolley heard people above and around him. There were others trapped nearby! He called out to them. The ability to talk to others gave him strength. But he had hurt his head and leg. It was dark and his glasses were gone. Even more terrifying was not knowing if anyone would rescue them. The earthquake had been massive. Other people were surely in worse shape.

"I just saw the walls rippling and just explosive sounds all around me. It all happened incredibly fast."

DAN WOOLLEY

debris—the scattered pieces of something that has been broken or destroyed

Hours after the earthquake, Woolley heard rescue workers. One of the people trapped near him was **evacuated**. The rescue workers said they would be back for him and the others, but hours passed and no one came. Woolley was sure they had forgotten about him. He had his journal with him. By the light on his cell phone, he wrote a goodbye letter to his two sons and his wife, Christina. He was convinced he would die waiting for help.

Finally, Woolley heard a shout from above. It was an American firefighter named Sam Gray, who was working with a team of French rescuers. Gray said he was coming. Soon Gray appeared, **rappelling** carefully down the ruined shaft with water and medical supplies. He gave Woolley water and treated his wounds. Gray then looked for a way to get Woolley out. Cutting a hole in the wall would take many hours — too long. Gray had no choice but to use the narrow and dangerous elevator shaft. He hooked Woolley to a harness. The team raised him up slowly. Rescuers were waiting along the way to help him navigate the metal spikes poking out and the sharp corners. Finally, Woolley reached the top and was carried to a van, which drove him to the hospital.

Rescue workers use rapelling gear to safely lower themselves into some areas.

evacuate—to leave a dangerous place to go somewhere safer

rappel—to slide down a strong rope

Rescue workers from around the world hurried to Haiti to help find victims after the 2010 earthquake.

CHAPTER 2

Catastrophe in California

The 1994 earthquake in Los Angeles ripped apart major
freeways, including the Newhall Pass Interchange.
In total, the quake caused nine freeway bridges to fall.

The 1994 Los Angeles earthquake destroyed thousands of buildings and injured more than 9,000 people.

In the early morning of January 14, 1994, Alan Hemsath woke to the sound of the earth exploding. Suddenly, his bedroom window shattered. The beams above him burst apart. He tried to run, but the ground was shaking. Somehow he ended up in his kitchen. The walls crashed down and pinned him to the floor.

Twenty other people were inside their apartments at Northridge Meadows in Los Angeles, California. Hemsath didn't know who was still alive. He called out for help. Someone answered and said they'd be back with rescuers. Hemsath waited. His leg and arm were wedged under debris. There were terrifying **aftershocks** that rumbled on and on.

At a fire station near Northridge Meadows, firefighter Mike Henry was shaken out of his bed by the earthquake. He and his crew jumped into their **turnouts** and boots, and hurried out in their fire engine.

aftershock—a small earthquake that follows a larger one

turnout—the protective clothing worn by firefighters, also known as bunker gear

When they arrived at Northridge Meadows, they were shocked. The top floors had flattened on top of Hemsath and several other residents. It took the crew several hours to find a way to reach Hemsath. When they did, they needed special tools to get him out. Hemsath's leg was freed of the beam that had fallen on it. But an electrical box was pinning his arm. The firefighters thought they might have to **amputate** Hemsath's arm. Finally, they were able to wedge an airbag under the box. Henry filled the airbag with air, which pushed up the electrical box. This made just enough room so that Hemsath could wiggle free.

"The whole valley was just pitch black. Dead, dead, dead black."

MIKE HENRY

Staying Safe During a Quake

- **If you feel an earthquake**: The safest thing to do is stop, cover your head and neck, and wait until the shaking stops. Protect your head and neck with your arms or a pillow, and try to get as low to the floor as possible.

- **If you are in a house**: Try to get to a corner away from windows or doors. Stay away from things that can fall on you. If you are in bed, stay there and cover your head and neck with your pillow. Do not try to hide under your bed or run outside.

- **If you are in a car**: Stop driving and stay put. Avoid parking beneath telephone wires or overpasses.

- **If you are already outside**: Move away from streetlights, buildings, and concrete. Try to get onto grass or dirt. Then drop, cover, and wait until the shaking stops.

amputate—to cut off someone's arm, leg, or other body part, usually because the part is damaged

A total of 60 people died in the 6.7-magnitude quake in Los Angeles in 1994.

CHAPTER 3

Town Reduced to Rubble

Earthquake rescue dogs can search an area for survivors much faster than a human.

In a small mountain town outside of Rome, Italy, a powerful earthquake struck at 3:36 a.m. on August 24, 2016. A second quake hit at 4:33 a.m. A 10-year-old girl named Giulia was in her two-story house. The walls collapsed on top of her, trapping her in a pile of rubble.

The town of Amatrice was flattened by the earthquake. Fire departments, police officers, and rescue workers hurried to the area to help find and rescue trapped people. Search-and-rescue officer Davide Agrestini arrived at 9:30 a.m. with his rescue dog, Sarotti.

The two searched the **wreckage** all day. Then Sarotti started to bark. When a rescue dog barks, it means that someone is alive and close to the surface. Agrestini and other rescue workers started to dig by hand. They saw cloth that looked like a kid's pajamas. It was Giulia. They kept digging and were able to pull her out. She had been beneath the ruins of her house, unable to move for 15 hours, but she was not hurt.

"The aim now is to save as many lives as possible. There are voices under the rubble; we have to save the people there."

SERGIO PIROZZI
MAYOR OF AMATRICE

"Sniffer" Rescue Dogs

Rescue dogs help find buried people after earthquakes. They can "sniff out" a buried person in seconds. But having a good nose isn't enough to be a rescue dog. They must be smart, **obedient**, and strong. They also have to learn special skills, such as how to ride in a helicopter, how to signal when someone is alive, and how to work in tight spaces. At the end of their training, each dog must pass strict tests.

wreckage—the broken remains of a vehicle or building that has been badly damaged or destroyed

obedient—able to follow rules and commands

CHAPTER 4

Chaos in Christchurch

The 6.3-magnitude earthquake in Christchurch, New Zealand, destroyed the Pyne Gould Guinness building, killing 18 people.

Ann Bodkin was in her office building in Christchurch, New Zealand, on February 22, 2011, when a powerful earthquake hit. The building shook violently and Bodkin realized the quake was going to be a big one. She tried to dive under her desk. Before she could get there, she was hit by falling pieces of the ceiling. Just as she got under the desk and lay flat, the rest of the ceiling came down. The desk **crumpled** on top of Bodkin, but it held up just enough to not crush her.

Bodkin tried to reach her cell phone. But it had been on her desk and was buried somewhere in the rubble. She could move her arms and legs a little bit. She could still breathe. Bodkin was unhurt, but she didn't know if anyone would find her.

Dozens of rescue workers searched for survivors in the collapsed Pyne Gould Guinness building. Ann Bodkin was saved after being trapped for 24 hours.

crumple—to become wrinkled or bent

Rescue workers sometimes use heavy machinery to remove layers of rubble. They must work carefully so that the pile doesn't shift and crush survivors waiting for rescue.

Rescuers had been working in Bodkin's building through the night, digging out survivors. They did not know that Bodkin was alive. Then they heard her shout. It took rescuers three hours to break through the broken walls and rubble to get close to Bodkin. Using many different types of drills, they broke through into the small space where Bodkin was trapped. They used a stick to pass her a bottle of water. Then they carefully cut a hole in the wall to free her. A violent aftershock shook the ruined building as Bodkin was being moved. She likely made it out in the nick of time.

"I started calling out to see if anyone else was around, but there was only silence. If I hadn't been crouching under the desk, I might not have survived."

ANN BODKIN

Measuring Earthquake Strength

Scientists use a seismograph to help them decide the strength of an earthquake. A seismograph records the size of the **vibrations** caused by the earthquake. The bigger the vibrations, the higher the magnitude. Magnitude is measured on a numerical scale.

About 900,000 minor earthquakes occur every year. These earthquakes have a magnitude of less than 2.5. They are rarely felt by people. There are about 500 moderate earthquakes per year. These quakes cause only small damage to buildings. Major earthquakes with a magnitude of 7 and higher can destroy entire towns.

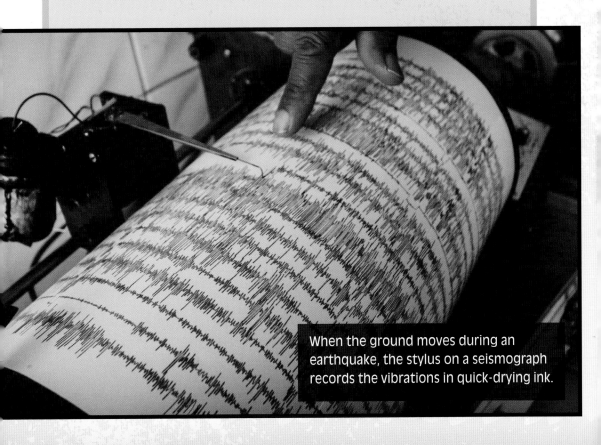

When the ground moves during an earthquake, the stylus on a seismograph records the vibrations in quick-drying ink.

vibration—a fast movement back and forth

CHAPTER 5
Coastal Town Flattened

In Tonsupa, a coastal town in Ecuador, residents tried to recover their belongings from the wreckage of a 7.8-magnitude earthquake in April 2016.

Ecuadoran and Colombian firefighters searched debris by hand, looking for survivors of the 2016 earthquake in Ecuador.

On April 16, 2016, in Portoviejo, Ecuador, hotel manager Pablo Cordova was on the fourth floor of the hotel where he worked when an earthquake struck. The hotel collapsed around him, burying him in concrete. Once the shaking stopped, he tried to call for help on his cell phone, but there was no service. He waited, hoping someone would come.

Cordova's wife was also waiting. She had heard about the earthquake, and was hoping to get word that he was alive. But hours passed. She learned that the hotel where Cordova worked had collapsed. She gave up. No one could survive such a disaster. Cordova's wife and boss started to plan his funeral.

Earthquake rescuers sometimes use power tools, such as saws and drills.

More than 30 hours passed, and Cordova was still alive. He prayed that he would live, and he was so thirsty that he drank his own urine. Finally, after 36 hours of waiting and hoping, he heard workers sorting through the rubble. He shouted for them, but they couldn't hear him. They were using digging machines to move debris. Cordova tried his cell phone again. It worked! He called his sister and told her where to find him.

A team of local rescuers was **on-site** when they received word that someone was alive inside. They stopped their machinery so they could hear him. After an hour of using saws and drills, they reached Cordova. They put him on a **backboard** and carried him out. He raised his hand in a wave of thanks as he was carried to the ambulance.

"They were organizing the funeral, but I've been reborn. I will have to give that coffin back because I still have a long way to go before I die."

PABLO CORDOVA

on-site—at an exact place

backboard—a large board used to carry people who are hurt and cannot walk

Make a Survival Kit

Scientists cannot predict earthquakes. Earthquakes can strike almost anywhere and at any time. The best way to prepare for an earthquake is to create a survival kit. Store survival items in a waterproof box or bag that can be easily found in an emergency. There should be enough supplies for everyone in the group to last three days. Take special care when packing important medicines, especially for those with life-threatening conditions. A basic kit should have:

- 1 gallon (3.8 liters) of water per person per day
- ready-to-eat foods that won't spoil, such as snack bars, cereal, and powdered milk
- first aid kit
- flashlight and extra batteries
- battery-powered or hand-cranked radio
- important medicines

CHAPTER 6

Nepal's Deadliest Earthquake

In the city of Kathmandu, Nepal, more than 600,000 buildings were damaged or destroyed in the 2015 earthquake.

The 2015 earthquake in Nepal caused avalanches on Mount Everest that killed 22 climbers.

Near the capital city of Kathmandu, Nepal, a giant earthquake struck in the middle of the day on April 25, 2015. The 7.8-magnitude quake flattened villages. It caused avalanches on Mount Everest and old temples were destroyed. More than 9,000 people died.

Teenager Pemba Lama was at work in a nine-story hotel in Kathmandu when the shaking started. He rushed downstairs. Then everything came crashing down. When he woke up, he found himself in a tiny space between a motorcycle and the fallen hotel floors. He was uninjured, but he could not move. The hours turned into days. He lay there, waiting. A container of butter was nearby and he ate every last bit. He also found a wet cloth and squeezed water from it to drink. He slept, only to wake up and wonder if he was dead. He had nightmares. Sometimes he heard voices talking to him. He didn't know if they were real.

Californian fire captain Andrew Olvera had been in Kathmandu for five days. He and his team from Los Angeles had been **scouting** the streets for survivors. They had not found any yet. Many people had died. He and his team of rescuers were working at a nearby bus station when they were told a voice was calling out from under a collapsed hotel. Someone beneath the rubble was alive!

Rescue teams from the United States worked with Nepalese army forces to rescue 15-year-old Pemba Lama.

scout—to look or search for something

Pemba Lama was trapped for 120 hours in the rubble of the 2015 earthquake in Kathmandu.

The team rushed to the hotel with search dogs and special tools, including jackhammers, saws, and cameras. The place where Lama was buried was very unstable. After three hours, rescuers had cleared a tunnel through the debris. A police officer was able to crawl in and strap Lama to a backboard. Then, as the crowd outside cheered, Lama was carried from the ruins and taken to a hospital.

"It's dangerous, but it's what we do. It's risk versus gain. To save a human life, we will risk almost everything."

ANDREW OLVERA

Glossary

aftershock (AF-tur-shok)—a small earthquake that follows a larger one

amputate (AM-pyuh-tayt)—to cut off someone's arm, leg, or other body part, usually because the part is damaged

backboard (BAK-bord)—a large board used to carry people who are hurt and cannot walk

crumple (KRUMP-uhl)—to become wrinkled or bent

debris (duh-BREE)—the scattered pieces of something that has been broken or destroyed

obedient (oh-BEE-dee-uhnt)—able to follow rules and commands

on-site (on-SITE)—at an exact place

rappel (ruh-PEL)—to slide down a strong rope

scout (SKOWT)—to look or search for something

tectonic plate (tek-TON-ik PLAYTE)—a gigantic slab of Earth's crust that moves around on the mantle

tsunami (tsoo-NAH-mee)—a gigantic ocean wave created by an undersea earthquake, landslide, or volcanic eruption

turnout (TURN-owt)—the protective clothing worn by firefighters, also known as bunker gear

vibration (vye-BRA-shuhn)—a fast movement back and forth

wreckage (REK-ij)—the broken remains of a vehicle or building that has been badly damaged or destroyed

Read More

Brennan, Linda Crotta. *We Have Earthquakes*. Tell Me Why. Ann Arbor, Mich.: Cherry Lake Publishing, 2015.

Freeburg, Jessica. *Collapse and Chaos: the Story of the 2010 Earthquake in Haiti*. Tangled History. North Mankato, Minn.: Capstone Press, 2017.

Furgang, Kathy. *Everything Volcanoes and Earthquakes*. Washington, D.C.: National Geographic, 2013.

Winchester, Simon. *When the Earth Shakes: Earthquakes, Volcanoes, and Tsunamis*. New York: Viking, 2015.

Internet Sites

Use FactHound to find Internet sites related to this book.

Visit *www.facthound.com*

Just type in 9781543501148 and go.

Check out projects, games and lots more at
www.capstonekids.com

Index